The Grass is Greener on This Side of the Fence!

Rob Vivian

Printed in Canada

ISBN 978-0-9950311-0-4

FIN 23 02 2016

Acknowledgements

I would like to acknowledge my Mom, Fran, for teaching me how to respect others and to always look on the lighter side of life; my Dad, Stormin Norm, for teaching me how to pick up girls; my wife, Coleen, who is awesome; my kids, Josh & Corissa, who are amazing; and my siblings, Randy, Rick, Norma & Eric, together we figured the trick to getting along ~ move out early and don't live close by.

A special thanks goes out to Karen Kettle for her editing suggestions.

And I want to express my gratitude for the many people along the way that have inspired me. There are too many of you to mention by name, but you know who you are!

Contents

One: *The River of Your Life* 1

Two: *The Attracter Factor* 11

Three: *Everyone has Two Lists* .21

Four: *The Journey is as much Fun as the Destination* 33

Five: *The Cows are Out* 43

Six: *Burn the Boats* 51

Seven: *It's Lonely at the Bottom* 59

Eight: *Make them Proud* 69

Nine: *The Scarecrow* 81

Ten: *You Can't put the Toothpaste Back in the Tube* 93

Eleven: *You Don't have to go from Zero to Hero* 101

Twelve: *The Locomotive* 111

Final Thoughts 123

Introduction

As we travel through this amazing thing we call life one thing is for sure, there are going to be a lot of ups and downs. The road of life is a maze of twists and turns and it's very easy to lose your way. You may suddenly feel lost and look around and wonder where you are and how you got there. I hope this book will act as a compass to guide you when you run into the bumps of life.

I believe that looking at the lighter side of life with joy and gratitude is a great mindset for a journey. The stories and illustrations in this book are life lessons that I've learned along the way. I can't say that I aced all the lessons that found me. The truth is they hit home with me mostly because they aced me. Sometimes we learn the most when things don't go as planned.

Nevertheless the past does not equal the future. Whatever you have or have not done in your life up to this point has little bearing on where you are heading. I'm a perfect example of this principle. I was by far the worst student in the history of the Toronto school system! Seeing as the system and I were diametrically opposed we decided to part ways when I was 15 years old. Of course, like all 15 year olds I knew everything. Looking back I now realize I actually knew less than nothing, if that's possible. So off into the maze of life I went making mistakes left and right. However over time the content of this book, principles and ideas that lead to success, came to me. Some would say I learned street smarts at the *School of Hard Knocks* and others would say I just got lucky in life. Neither is entirely true. Life doesn't play favourites. If you do it right you get good results; if you don't, you don't. The concepts in this book will work regardless of your education. There is wisdom to be found outside of school. Don't get me wrong; if I could do it over I would definitely do it differently. I would be the total opposite. I'd strive to be the best student not the worst. However once something is in the past, it's in the past. The most important question is, "What are you going to do now?"

Enjoy
Rob Vivian

The Grass is Greener on This Side of the Fence!

One

The River of Your Life

Visualize yourself standing on the shore of a big river. It's very wide and very deep. This river is the river of your life. As you stand there, you notice the current is flowing to your left. Glancing downstream to the left, you see sharp rocks, rough water, and rapids. "I don't want to go down there," you think to yourself. As you glance to your right you discover a pleasant surprise. Off in the distance you see your goals, the thriving business you've been dreaming about, that 'in shape' body you would love to have, and the supportive relationships you desire.

You instantly realize that achieving your goals, those goals you see off in the distance, is going to require a lot of effort. You're going to have to get wet, all the while avoiding the rocks and rough water. With a big splash, into the water you go. It's time to go swimming. As you tread water, looking back at your entry point, you realize you've been here before. This isn't the first time you've started this quest. As you stare back at the shore, doubts

1

begin to creep into your mind, "Do I really want to start this adventure. After all, my life is pretty good. I'm in average shape. I have average relationships and my income is average... well to be honest, below average. Things aren't so bad. Are they? Who am I fooling... things definitely need to change! I've been living a mediocre life for quite some time." With determination and resolve you begin to swim...stroke, stroke, breathe, stroke, stroke, breathe. You remember that quote from that motivational CD you've been listening to, **"Every journey begins with a single step."** ~ *Maya Angelou.* In this case, it begins with a single stroke.

Once and for all you're on your way, your way to accomplishing something important. It may not be important at a world changing level, but it's important to you. Stroke, stroke, stroke, swim, swim, and swim some more. Don't forget to breathe. You're on your way to a worthwhile cause. Finally once and for all, you're going to achieve those things you've been dreaming about for most of your life. You're headed towards your goals... to have a thriving business that you're proud of, to be in the physical shape you've always dreamed of, to have time for family and friends, and to be recognized as a leader in your field. Another quote from that CD you've been listening to pops into your head, **"Always do your best!"** ~ *Miguel Ruiz.* That's the quote that brought you to the river in the first place. You want to give it your all! Stroke, stroke, and breathe.

Now's the time to let you know you're not the first person to embark on this journey. Everyone has his or her own life river. As a matter of fact, millions of people jump into the water every day and start to swim towards their goals.

So the question is, why are so few successful? Why do so few accomplish their goals and achieve their dreams? What is it that gets in the way? What prevents them from accomplishing their goals? Why is it that they fall short almost every time?

Good questions! Thanks for asking.

The problem is the current is flowing in the wrong direction. Each stroke is a struggle. Wouldn't it be great if the current were flowing toward your goals instead of against your efforts? Think about it, it's a huge challenge to gain ground on your goals. You work really hard mustering massive amounts of energy and enthusiasm coupled with a healthy dose of commitment. You put your head down and swim. You look up and you've actually gained ground. **GOOD JOB!** However, you notice that every time you rest, every time you tread water you lose ground to the river. It's relentless. Every time you take a break to catch your breath the current thrusts you back down the river closer to rocks and the turbulent water. So you think, "Wouldn't it be great if the current flowed towards my goal instead of pushing me down river in the direction of all that danger and disappointment?"

What an awesome thought!

Here's another key question, "Why is my river flowing in the wrong direction?" After all, it's the river of my life... not someone else's river. The interesting thing about your river is it actually started out neutral, calm. Your mindset dictates the direction of the current: what you ponder all day, that nagging little voice in your head, and how you spin things influences the direction of the water flow. Are you a glass half empty or a glass half full kind of guy or gal? Once again, the CD you've been listening to pops into your head with another insightful quote "**You become what you think about.**" ~ *Earl Nightengale.* At the end of the day, that statement is absolutely true. It's not "you become what you **should** think about," or "you become what you **want** to think about," it's "you become what you **do** think about."

Wait a minute. It's hard to imagine that you would create a strong current to hinder your progress and put your dreams and aspirations in jeopardy, but millions of people do it every day. You may not realize you're sabotaging your own efforts. However let's be clear, that's exactly what's happening. It's you, all you. No other person has the authority to tamper with your river, just you and only you. The world may put obstacles in your path but you can choose to flow around them. To change the direction of the current, you have to choose to be positive. You have to discipline yourself to think positive thoughts. You become what you think about. Get your day flowing in the right direction by saying some positive affirmations!

Something awesome is going to happen today.
I gain energy as the day goes by.
I am youthful and vibrant.
I'm alive excited and full of energy.

Saying affirmations like these every morning 10 to 15 times will get your head in the right place. You can, of course, use other positive affirmations of your own that are more personal or specific to you. Then purposefully make these affirmations your self-talk all day long.

After a couple of days you'll notice the current slowing down somewhat. Keep it up. It won't be long until the current comes to a complete stop and then slowly begins flowing in the opposite direction. That's right the current will actually be flowing toward your goals. **THAT'S EXCITING!**

Unfortunately most folks don't start their day by filling their heads with positive thoughts; instead they focus on what's not working in their lives and businesses. The interesting thing is the desire to achieve their goals is still intact. Unfortunately the current of their negativity is just too strong. Every day they venture out, muster up all their earthly energy, dive back into the river and start swimming while the whole time thinking this probably isn't going to work. Faster and faster the current presses against them. Finally one day, before they drown, they crawl out of the river for good. Despite their efforts they may be close to where they started or they may have been swept down the river a ways closer to the danger.

They say to themselves, "That's it. I give up. I've had enough. I'm done." That day is the end of their dreams, the end of those things they wanted so badly: a thriving business, healthy relationships, and the desire to be in peak physical condition. This is a very sad day and unfortunately the likely outcome for most folks

So the question you should be asking is...?

Are you saying, "Can I avoid this disaster if I discipline myself to fill my head with positive thoughts every day?" The answer to that question is absolutely, unequivocally YES. Your mindset will dictate which direction the current is flowing and the speed of the water.

> **"As a man thinketh in his heart, so is he."**
> **~ *Proverbs 23:7***

Sometimes in life, solutions seem simple... sometimes too simple for us to accept. But there it is. After two decades of coaching and training business leaders in personal development, I've noticed it's difficult for them to accept this simple reality. They're looking for something more complicated, something with more steps ~ perhaps a 10 point plan! The reality is your control of your thinking or the lack there of dictates whether you swim against the current in life or turn the tide and let the water speed your progress. I'm sure you know folks that have that luxury; everything seems to go their way. Notice those folks are the positive thinkers of the planet.

I'm not saying you're a negative person. Positive people have negative thoughts all the time. I certainly do! The trick is to have your positive thinking outweigh the negative. The river can't flow two directions at the same time. If positive thinking is dominant, life is better. If negative thinking is dominant life is harder. It's really that simple.

"Your expectations and your results always align perfectly."

In a nutshell

If you're a glass half full kind of guy or gal, you automatically spin things positively in your mind. If you're the type of person that's always looking on the bright side and seeing the silver lining in every cloud then you have the river of your life flowing in the correct direction. On the other hand if you tend to constantly view things from a negative perspective, a glass half empty kind of guy or gal, then unfortunately life will be a little more challenging. Better learn to be a great swimmer. You're going to need it. Given the two choices you might want to train your brain to see the positive in everything so life can become one big lazy river ride.

Helpful Exercise #1

Thinking negatively doesn't make you a negative person; it makes you a positive person that thinks negatively in some areas. However even though you're a positive person overall, those areas of negative thinking effect both the direction of the current in the river of your life and the current's intensity. The exercise below helps you to think differently about some of those areas.

Negative thoughts creep in when I think about:

Area of concern #1

_____

_____

Area of concern #2

_____

_____

Area of concern #3

_____

_____

Take a second look:

A positive spin on concern #1 is:

_____

_____

A positive spin on concern #2 is:

_____

_____

A positive spin on concern #3 is:

_____

_____

If we view it better it will be better.

You cannot swim to new horizons until you have the courage to lose sight of the shore.

William Faulkner

Two

The Attracter Factor

The purpose of this book, *The Grass is Greener on this Side of the Fence*, is to help people understand that they can have green grass all around them. In fact, with a positive attitude they can attract much more than green grass to their side of the fence.

As I travel around teaching seminars and coaching, I find there are a lot of folks who are not OK with who they are or where they are. Not OK with **where** you are I get that and I can help! We all want to be further down the path toward success. But I find it a tragedy that a person can spend their life not being happy with **who** they are. When you're not OK with who you are, it's like running in water, you can't go anywhere or certainly not in a hurry. When I see someone that is simply not content with who they are, my heart goes out to them. They have created a mental prison for themselves and it's time for them to break out. If you want to attract awesome things into your life on a regular basis you must be OK with who you are as a person. Luckily everyone holds the key to accepting who he or she is...the key to the door.

Consider that you're the only person on the planet with your fingerprints. It's hard to imagine when you look at your fingertips, that there are over seven billion different ways you can run those lines. That's shocking. You're also the only person on planet Earth with your DNA. Not even identical twins are truly identical because their environments affect how their DNA is expressed. As you process these two amazing realities a couple of things become glaringly obvious. First you're very special, and secondly you're unique. Think about it, you're the only person alive on the whole Earth with your fingerprints, and the only one with your DNA. This tells you that you're not an accident you're not here by chance. There's a bigger picture at play. You have meaning and value. You're here for a reason with something to contribute. Your life is a mission.

If my life had no direct meaning or absolute purpose my uniqueness would not be necessary. I would not need my own personal DNA or fingerprints I can call my own. If I wasn't important in the big scheme of things I could be a generic brand and I'm not. I'm important. I have a part to play, and I'm here for a reason. So are you! When an artist paints a picture, they often sell copies of them as numbered prints. They are signed and numbered 1/500, 2/500 and so on. I have several beautiful signed numbered prints in my house. You may have some too.

That's how it is with art but not humans. I am 1/1 just like you, you are 1/1 there are not 500 of me, or 500 of you, just one. You're an original, a masterpiece, and a true work of art!

The title of this chapter is, **The Attracter Factor.** Although I'm making the point that it's important that you're OK with **who** you are, it doesn't mean that you shouldn't purposefully attract awesome things into your life. Every person should always be on a quest to achieve more, to always, always, always do their best. If you are not OK with who you are, attracting amazing things into your life on a regular basis is basically impossible. Once you accept yourself, awesome things can flow effortlessly to you. The Law of Attraction has been around for a long time and many different people have written about it. It's not a scientific law but the idea that like attracts like. Positive thoughts and actions attract positive things.

When we're comfortable with who we are we experience a level of contentment, this contentment is necessary if we want to move forward and attract our desires into our life. Without this contentment we simply cannot move forward. It's like having an anchor attached to your leg. You're immobilised. You're stuck. It's sad to say that most of the population lives in this exact circumstance.

If this is you, I hope this chapter helps. Sometimes folks ask me, why should I do my best? I might fail. Why should I strive to achieve? What's the purpose? Well, because you can that's why. Think about it, if you can do something you should. Any positive thing that you have the ability to do, you should do. It's as simple as that. If you have the ability to make a positive difference and you don't, you'll probably regret it later.

When I was in my mid twenties, I was a youth leader at the church we attended. A couple of times a year we would take the youth group to a local seniors' home, and the youth would sing as a choir. I'm not sure we were very good but the residents loved it. I always found it interesting that in conversation with the elderly folks, they always shared with me the regrets they had in life. At the time I was 25 years old and it became very clear to me that these folks were not regretting what they had done in life but what they had not done. Obviously they had made some mistakes and done a few things in their lives that didn't make them proud. However, as they were approaching the end of their lives they were not focused on what they would like to undo. Instead, their regrets were all the things they had not done in the time that was allocated for them. We can learn a lot from our elders who have been calling Earth home for almost 100 years. They were teaching me that if I don't do things when I have a chance, if I don't use my time wisely, I'm going to regret it later on.

My business career started when I was 26 years old and the truth is the residents of that seniors' home inspired me. Every time we visited, they would always say the same thing not one or two, all of them. It's the things you didn't do, the opportunities that were there for you and you didn't do your best. Those are the things you will regret.

It's difficult if not impossible to attract good things into your life when you are not OK with who you are, and it's interesting that as soon as you're comfortable with who you are then good things come to you. In your mind's eye imagine a big bucket of metal shavings and then stick an electromagnetic pole into it. I'm sure you can visualize those metal shavings instantly clinging to that magnet. That's how quickly good things will come your way when your mind is in the right place accepting of who you are and open to receiving good things. Unfortunately if you're not OK with who you are then of course you cannot attract desirable things into your life the **"attracter factor"** is turned off. Visualize the same illustration this time but turn the power off so the pole is not magnetic. You stick it into the bucket of metal shavings and nothing sticks.

If you want the attracter factor to work for you, you need to have the right frame of mind; you need to be programmed to receive. Sometimes it's difficult for me to observe people who attend my seminars on multiple occasions and never really move forward or achieve anything significant. The truth is, unless they are OK with who they are; I can't really help them. They need to be square with themselves to have the power to magnetize the pole. This allows all of their heart's desires to flow to them.

At a seminar the other day, a nice young lady came up to me at the break and said, I'm starting to work on the Law of Attraction." Which wasn't my topic but I guess she had attended another seminar or had recently listened to a CD. Of course my seminar was somewhat motivational so I guess it kind of fit. Her statement was interesting "I'm starting to work on the Law of Attraction." The truth is we've all been using on the Law of Attraction all our lives. It's probably what we're best at. As a matter of fact, we are masters of the Law of Attraction. Everything that is prevalent in your life today is a projection of previous thoughts and everything that you think and ponder today will echo in your future. A positive, optimistic frame of mind will attract positive things while a negative attitude attracts more of the same.

There is a saying that the two things in life that are certain are death and taxes, add this topic to the list it's a guarantee. What this young lady really meant was I'm going to work on **attracting the right things** into my life. I'm going to control my thoughts and think good positive thoughts and attract good positive things into my life. Believe me when I tell you, "You're a master of the Law of Attraction you've been doing it your whole life. It might very well be the thing that you are the best at!"

In a nutshell

Not being OK with where you are in life is fine. The truth is most people shouldn't be OK with where they are. They should be much farther down the path to excellence. So wanting to get somewhere else is perfectly fine. It's probably a good idea. However not being OK with who you are, is a totally different situation. The truth is you are awesome and deep down you know this is true. It might be buried deep inside; maybe you haven't felt good about yourself for a while. However at your core you know you have a lot to offer, you bring a lot to the table of life. It's important that you get square with yourself in order to discover the awesome future that is patiently waiting for you.

Helpful Exercise #2

The more we think about something the greater the odds that we will attract that exact item into our lives. What we focus on we attract, positive thoughts become positive actions, and positive actions make our dreams come true.

What would you like to attract into your life?

Awesome thing #1

_____

_____

Awesome thing #2

_____

_____

Awesome thing #3

_____

_____

Write out the perfect thought to attract that awesome thing.

Awesome thought #1

_____

_____

Awesome thought #2

_____

_____

Awesome thought #3

_____

_____

What you think about comes about.

Welcome to planet Earth

there is nothing you cannot be or do, or have.

You have a magnificent creator

Abraham

Three

Everyone has Two Lists

Everyone has two lists, a list of what's going their way in business, family and relationships, and a list of things currently not going as planned. I know that sometimes it might seem that nothing is going your way and that it's just you. Somehow life's good for everyone but you, of course nothing could be further from the truth.

You're not alone. Everyone has two lists. There's a wise saying, "If we all threw our problems in a pile and saw everyone else's, we'd grab ours back." ~ Regina Brett. That's a good lesson to remember. It certainly helps keep our thinking in check.

So the question is why do people focus so much on what's not working for them instead of what is working in all the other aspects of life? Well that's a pretty good question! The answer is partly conditioning, let's face it the society we live in is less than a positive environment. Take the evening news as an example, on most evenings there's no shortage of natural disasters on the planet, not to mention all the cruel and devastating things human beings do to other human beings. If it bleeds, it leads. It's no surprise we tend to slip to looking at the negative side of things. Even something as simplistic as the weather report telling you there's a ten percent chance of rain can dampen the mood. Well I guess we're not going on a picnic this weekend it's going to rain! Why not advertise there is a ninety percent chance it will be dry. It might even be sunny. It's no wonder that in our mostly negative and slightly cynical society we tend to lean on the negative side of life or the list of what's not working.

Not everyone on the planet is on a quest of self-improvement, not everyone has goals, not everyone is on a mission for maximization. So if you're not interested in being your best if you don't mind being part of problem then none of this matters to you. However, if you do want to be part of the solution if you do want to reach your personal potential then it matters... it matters a lot, on an importance level it's up there with oxygen.

The truth is if you're not focused on what's working in all aspects of your life the chances of achieving your goals and making your dreams a reality are stacked heavily against you. So let's take a look at some practical things you can do to help you focus on what's working in your life and in turn assist you in achieving your personal optimum potential.

Read your gratitude list daily!

The first point would be, create a gratitude list. This is a very simple process with a high-octane result. You simply take a minute or two to write out eight to ten things for which you are grateful. If this is difficult you're thinking too much, it's as simple as:

I'm grateful for the country I live in.
I'm grateful for my family.
I'm grateful for my health.
I'm grateful for my job.
I'm grateful for my friends.
I'm grateful for my home.
I'm grateful for the food I eat.
I'm grateful for my car.
I'm grateful for those that fought for my freedom.

I heard a comedian say that he was grateful for water parks... they're a great place to be on a hot summer day. His joke was that some countries don't have enough fresh water to drink and we have so much we play in it. It was meant as a joke but it's also true. As you can see it's not difficult to come up with eight to ten things for which you're sincerely grateful. Simply jot these down on a piece of paper and keep the list on your nightstand. When you wake up in the morning your gratitude list will be right there to greet you.

As a business coach, I have assigned this exercise many times. When I inquire on the next coaching call about the homework assignment I get one of two responses. Response one is, "Yes I did. That was very powerful. Thank you. I can't believe how powerful that was to put those things that I'm grateful for in my mind first thing in the morning. My whole day seemed to take on a new perspective, I was definitely in a much better frame of mind and I had a better week!" Or I get the second response, "Well I was pretty busy this week. So I didn't have time to do that homework assignment." As the coach, you can't let people slide, so I always suggest we take a minute and write out some things that are on or would be on their gratitude list. It usually takes about two to three minutes and we have created an awesome gratitude list. So there you go the homework assignment that you didn't have time for last week has just been completed. The usual response is, "I guess I did have time for that assignment", to which I reply, "I guess you did. Not to worry it's now done."

As previously mentioned all you need to do is put your gratitude list on your nightstand and read it every morning. This is an excellent exercise to help you focus on what's working in your life. Putting things in your mind that you are most thankful for, as your first thoughts of the day. I have had several clients ask me if they should read their list on weekends or just workdays. Folks let's be honest it's only going to take ten seconds, do it every day. You want to be in the group that says, "Wow I can't believe how powerful that simple exercise is, that really helped me."

Affirmations are also a very powerful tool for assisting us in staying focused on the list of what's working for us and avoiding the list that's not. At a seminar the other day I had someone say to me that they don't believe in affirmations. I thought it was quite odd that someone would use an affirmation to say they don't believe in affirmations. An affirmation is simply affirming a thought or belief, nothing more or less than that. If you say, "I'm not a morning person," that's an affirmation. You're just affirming that you are not a morning person. I don't think we can really say we don't believe in affirmations. We could say that we don't believe in the power of affirming something. That I would accept. However if this is your position, believing that your words and thoughts do not play a part in the direction your life is heading; you're not really paying attention to what is happening in your life.

Everything in your life from your business, health, relationships and every other aspect of your life is 100% dictated by your thoughts and words. If you look at your life honestly, everything you really like and every area that you're excited about is going well because of your positive thoughts and affirmations about those areas. I would be willing to bet that all the areas that lack vibrancy in your life and the items on your list of things that are not going your way are still there because you are thinking and affirming negative thoughts and statements.

Affirmations are the self-talk your inner voice has you pondering all day long. Your self-talk is a lot more powerful than you think. I remember a specific client that joined our coaching program. His reason for joining was that he was massively in debt and he needed help to get out. That's a pretty good reason to get some help. On our first scheduled coaching call I inquired about what exactly is happening in his financial situation. His response was that there was about $300,000 in bad debt, credit cards and lines of credit. He wasn't too worried about his mortgage; it was his credit card debt that had him stressed out. Then he said something very interesting…he said, "I think all day long about the need to get out of debt." So I said, "John (not his real name) what you are thinking about all day long is debt, is that correct." John agreed but was quick to point out that he wasn't thinking about more debt but a healthy thought of less debt. I in return was quick to agree that that does kind of make sense, however his main train of thought was still debt! I could hear in John's voice that he was starting to get my point. I explained to John that if he thought about debt all day long even though his motive was correct, thinking about less debt was still thinking about debt all day long. It's really not a surprise that he was falling further and further into debt. We all ultimately become what we think.

If you don't believe me let me give you an example, something that we've all experienced that will clearly illustrate that you become what you think about. You're driving down a major highway beside a transport truck.

You're traveling in the same direction at the same speed. You look over at the truck for several seconds then straight ahead again. Instantly you notice that you have moved a foot or two towards the truck so you quickly correct your course. This is usually where your spouse gets angry with you. The truth is it's not your fault. You were simply moving toward something you focused on. Another example would be stock car racing on an oval track; as you know the drivers take their cars as fast as they can around the track. The object is to accomplish this and avoid all the dangers along the way. However, sometimes problems are unavoidable. The drivers are trained that if they are spinning out they are to look to the infield. As soon as the car begins to spin it automatically wants to go up the track into the wall. The drivers are trained to understand that if they look at the wall even though their desire is to not go into the wall they will go directly up the track and into the wall. The only chance they have is to look to the infield, focus on the infield and the car might follow. I realize these are very basic examples of how our focus dictates the direction of each and every aspect of our lives.

It's inevitable; you become what you think about. You go in the direction of your focus.

OK, back to John and his debt problem. As you can see, John focused on the wall when his problems started and up he went into the wall, or you can say he focused on the transport truck a little too long and had himself a mishap.

So what's John's solution? Well, John needs to look to the infield. John needs to ignore the wall even though it's an imminent problem. Once I explained this to John I could hear hope in his voice that the light at the end of the tunnel wasn't an oncoming train. John was ready to get started. It would have been too easy to tell him, "Just don't think about the debt." After all, thinking about the debt had become a habit, a bad habit. I explained to John that he needed to replace this thinking, this bad habit with some better thoughts, thoughts that are good habits that would create better results. For homework, John promised to include the following affirmations in his daily self-talk:

a) Something awesome is going to happen today.

b) Money comes to me and I am responsible with it.

c) I love helping others with my extra money.

John was quick to point out that he didn't have enough money for himself right now never mind others. I asked John if he would like these three things to be true. He thought for a second then said, "Of course, I would love something awesome to happen every day and to have money come to me and be responsible with it. The truth is I would love to help others with my excess cash, as a matter of fact, I have been very generous in the past." So together we decided to make these three thoughts the infield on John's racetrack of life. He agreed to focus on these thoughts and let them become his reality. At the writing of this chapter, John has been in our coaching about one year, I can't tell you that John is already out of debt however $100,000 has been paid off and the other $200,000 should take about two years. John is sliding away from the wall and into the infield.

I would like to share a couple of side notes to this story. The joy for John didn't come when all the debt was gone… it began as soon as John was clear that this would work. So John has been living for one year now with the weight of the world off his shoulders. It was especially nice when John's wife called to thank me for getting her husband back, she missed the vibrant guy he use to be and was happy to be reunited with him again. Interestingly, John has started eating right and working out again. So what really happened here? Well just a little shift. John was focused on what was not working in his life instead of what was working. He just needed to shift his thinking. Many of you reading this book are in the exact situation. You've just made a common mistake, the good news is it's easy to fix. Why not write a couple of good affirmations and make them your self-talk. I guarantee whatever you tell yourself all day long will become your reality. Your life will begin to go in that direction.

There's really no disputing this idea. The principle is absolute. I've heard people say that's just what you motivational self-help speakers and coaches say… it's not really true. Well you must understand that this principle isn't something pedaled the last 100 years or so by ambitious folks, this principle has been around a lot longer than that. As a matter of fact it's a proverb. **"As a man thinketh in his heart so is he"** ~ Proverbs 23:7. In other words what you really believe in your heart that's the direction your life is going period.

It's been said that your future is an echo of your thoughts today and that everything you have and are today is a projection of your thoughts in the past. I agree!

In a nutshell

Everyone has a list of what's going their way and a list of what's not. Everyone, me you and all 7 billion people that occupy this planet have two lists. The problem is most folks spend all day pondering the list of things that are currently not going their way. At this point you should be pretty clear how the law of attraction works, so focusing all day on what's not going your way is going to have a predictable result. You're going to get more of the same. However every coin has two sides so investing your energies all day long with a direct focus pondering those 8 or 10 things that are going your way will, of course, generate the same predictable result. You're going to get more of the same! I would highly recommend that you accentuate the positive.

Helpful Exercise #3

I mentioned the gratitude list in this chapter. It is probably one of the most powerful exercises a person can do to affect their mind in a positive manner. Take a few minutes and jot down the top 10 things that you are grateful for.

I AM GRATEFUL FOR:

Items

1) _____

2) _____

3) _____

4) _____

5) _____

6) _____

7) _____

8) _____

9) _____

10) _____

Expressing your gratitude makes a difference in your attitude.
Read your list every day.

Entrepreneurship is living

a few years of your life

like most people won't,

so that you can spend the rest of your life

like most people can't.

Unknown

Four

The Journey is as Much Fun as the Destination

As I've travelled around North America for the last 20 years or so teaching seminars and speaking at conventions I see folks in a desperate attempt to get somewhere, somewhere fun, somewhere exciting, somewhere fulfilling. I've seen the same trend on the 50,000 plus coaching calls that I have personally facilitated. The idea, that the journey is as much fun as the destination, is a problem for a lot of people.

From my perspective, many of these folks who are desperately trying to get somewhere else are already in a good place. As I interact with them I see awesome people with supportive families. I see healthy, vibrant people living in a great country. They drive nice cars and have comfortable homes. However, many of these people are urgently trying to get somewhere else. Now I'm not saying that we shouldn't have goals or have a strong desire to better our position in life. We should, of course. As a matter of fact that's exactly what I do for a living. I spend the majority of my waking hours thinking of ideas, illustrations and inspirational stories to assist others to be the best they can. To help them attain all of their aspirations, I often remind them that most of the elements that make up this awesome future are already in place. Everything isn't in the future. However if we spend all our time thinking and dreaming about what could be in the future and not acknowledging what we currently have we're making a major mistake. Should we add awesome things in our future, of course we should! But, we shouldn't be so focussed on those awesome things that we ignore the incredible things that are currently going on around us.

I know this is an over used saying, but we need to "**stop and smell the roses.**" There are areas of our lives that are currently amazing. If we stop to acknowledge them on a regular basis we will make the journey as much fun as the destination. If we ignore what is wonderful in our current life and spend all our time thinking and dreaming about what could be in the future, we blind ourselves to the little joys and successes along the way. Some people invest their entire lives dreaming about what they wished they had and never take the time to appreciate what's all around them.

I have the honour of working with many incredible clients. My goal with everyone is to be a mentor so they can be the best that they can be in every area of their lives. My goal is to guide them in achieving a lot more than just profits for their bank accounts. I do my very best to help them become architects in every aspect of their lives. My observation in this endeavour is that many of my clients are not enjoying the process, and quite frankly I think they should. Again, the journey is as much fun as the destination. Success isn't about getting somewhere it's about enjoying the road along the way. Think about it. What makes a person successful? Do they have to have it all? No. The truth is if you are currently prospering in something you are successful at least in that area of your life. You might not be where you want to be YET, but you're on the right track.

Let's use your weight as an example. One of the top ten things people worry about is their weight. So let's say right now you're in dreadful shape! Even going to the fridge for something stuffed with delicious calories is exhausting. You're fifty pounds overweight and you avoid looking at yourself in the mirror. Your doctor is warning you that serious health issues are on the horizon. I think you'd agree that if this is you, you're currently not experiencing success as far as your physical weight is concerned. Obviously you want to drop those fifty pounds, regain your youthful energy levels and hear your doctor say your health is in order. You can imagine reaching your goal. With it achieved, life would take a positive turn for you. Every day would be a new day full of positive opportunities. This one change could make a dramatic improvement. It would be big, really big.

If you could do this, you would have definitely reached your goal. You would have climbed the mountain and in doing so charted a new course for your future. You know this achievement will require a lot discipline, persistence and a massive commitment on your part. That's what achieving goals is all about. I'm sure it's clear to you what I'm talking about. Think back. At some point, you've already exercised that kind of commitment to achieve something or the discipline required got the better of you. Either way you're clear about the required commitment. **"A river cuts through stone not by its power but by its persistence."** The river was successful not from its power but from its persistence, persistence is the key. The river kept at it and eventually achieved success. Now obviously it's different for us, the river doesn't have the emotions and temptations we have but the principle is the same. It takes a huge amount of self-discipline to conquer the urges to eat the wrong foods and to find the time and energy to exercise. Most folks fail in their attempt to get in better shape. They just can't seem to muster up as much persistence as the river. Getting in shape is not a trivial goal. Achieving success in this area of your life is more than just improving your appearance; it also has many health benefits. We all get news from our doctors and the better shape we're in the better the news gets.

The reason most folks fail to get in better shape is that they don't view the process correctly. They're too hard on themselves. Is it really realistic to accomplish something of this magnitude without slip ups or the occasional slide backwards? The answer is no. The trick for success is to think realistically and factor in a margin for error. I always teach that 80% of anything is a lot. Eating 80% of the right foods or completing 80% of your scheduled workouts is a huge step forward. So don't be so hard on yourself. If you're really trying to accomplish something significant in your life, work on the 80% rule. So imagine you stick at it... at least 80% of the time. In 6 to 12 months you'll see a significant upgrade in your health and lifestyle. Congratulations! You will receive good news from your doctor. You can shop for new clothes and yes, skinny jeans are once again a possibility, maybe for the first time since you were a teenager. **I'm not saying skinny jeans are a good idea I'm just saying its good they're an option.**

The question is when was the success achieved? Was it when you reached your target weight? Was it the first time you pulled on those skinny jeans? Or did you achieve success when you lost that first pound? I believe you reached success even earlier! You were successful as soon as you started eating the right foods 80% of the time and completing 80% of your scheduled work out routines. You didn't look any different in the mirror and you probably felt worse. You might have had some aching muscles in places you didn't even know existed... but those were all signs of success. They were things to be celebrated. Right at that point you had success, you may or may not have had success the following week but no one can take the first week's success away from you. The point is that success starts in week one. You have accomplished a victory in this one area of your life. The light at the end of the tunnel is no longer an oncoming train.

The trick of course is being persistent, just like the river. You succeed one day at a time. Over time things will improve until the goal has been attained. The final result will be amazing of course, but that's not when the success appears. You were successful in week one and you should celebrate it. **The journey is as much fun as the destination.** If you're only happy when you achieve your ultimate goal, how are you going to stick with the plan through the tough times? It becomes difficult to forgive yourself when you falter because success is even further away. But if you build in a 20% margin for error and you celebrate each little victory you can keep moving forward.

Most folks never really achieve the aspiration of being their absolute best. When they look at what they're trying to accomplish, it feels like such a daunting task, it's not even within the realm of possibility. The success seems too far away and the challenges insurmountable. All it takes is a change of mindset. You can push yourself to give 80% this week. We can deal with next week next week. You can have big dreams but keep your focus on doing one thing at a time. It's so much easier to accomplish small tasks. Go one week at a time and be happy with your success. When you look at it this way anyone who can put four weeks of 80% in a row is a lot more likely to be successful in week five, than the person that looks at success being the final result, which is a distant finish line.

Anything you were able to achieve 80% of the time this week was a victory. Nobody is expecting 100% from you; nobody is expecting perfection from you. Nobody is expecting you to tackle improving all aspects of your life at once. I hope you're not expecting perfection from yourself. That's a bit misguided. So pick a place to start. If you honestly try your best in any area of your life achieving 80% is attainable. Start small and celebrate as you go. Enjoy feeling satisfaction and a sense of accomplishment. 80% isn't so difficult after all.

In this chapter, we've considered getting in shape, but you can insert your own challenge. The process is the same for every issue, if you can master your challenge 80% of the time this week, then you can do it again next week. Enjoy yourself. **The journey in life is as much fun as the destination.** Success is a small series of achievements. You're going from one scenic lookout on the road to the next. Enjoy the process not just the end result. Make sure every week you're travelling somewhere you want to go!

There is no doubt we should have aspirations and dreams for the future, and make plans to achieve them. Just not at the expense of an awesome today!

In a nutshell

The journey of life is what life is all about... not the ending. We all know how that's going to work out. A group of people will gather and pay their final respects. The true enjoyment and fulfilment of life happens day to day. Each day gives you the chance to be your very best in every aspect of life. So take time every day to enjoy all the wonder around you. You're a pilgrim creating new paths as you go. Along the way you'll achieve lots of goals, and gain satisfaction from what you've accomplished. That feeling won't be new to you it will be put alongside all the joy and fulfilment you gained along the way. **The journey is as much fun as the destination**

Helpful Exercise #4

Enjoying life along the way is the trick to finding fulfillment. If you find a person that is driven to succeed and content all at the same time, you've found the person everyone wants to be around. You've found a leader.

Write down three areas of your life that you are really enjoying right now. Don't focus on accomplishments or things. Focus on processes. When you're happy, what are you doing?

I'm happy when I'm:

_____

_____

I'm happy when I'm:

_____

_____

I'm happy when I'm:

_____

_____

Life is as much about the today
as it is about the someday!

It's your road and your road alone,

others can walk it with you

but no one can walk it for you.

Unknown

Five

The Cows Are Out

What you focus on expands in your mind! We all get down on ourselves, I mean really down on ourselves when we've had a lapse of judgment and done something we shouldn't have done. Let's face it we're not always the voice of reason. Maybe you made a mistake consciously or subconsciously… either way… something has happened and it has you down in the dumps. Or you didn't do something that you know you should have done. It was your responsibility, it needed to get done, and you were clearly the person that needed to make it happen… and you didn't. The reason at this point doesn't matter. You screwed up.

Once things are done, they're done. If you made a mistake, dwelling on it serves no positive purpose at all. **What you focus on expands in your mind!** You screwed up. It's best to start looking for a solution. Dwelling on your error, misjudgement, or screw up will actually make matters worse. If you dwell on the mistake it expands in your mind. It get's bigger and bigger and worse and worse as you roll it over and over again in your brain. Soon it occupies all your headspace. Have you ever seen time-lapse nature photography on television? It speeds images up so you can watch a flower bloom in just seconds. That's how fast a negative thought can take root, gain an identity, create mass in your thoughts, and develop a life of its own. This thing that's occurred needs a solution not an address of its own!

A negative thought can create a home in your mind and a life of its own so quickly it's scary. It has the ability to take root, grow and fester. It can actually shut you down and immobilize you in no time at all. A negative thought, full blown in your mind, can have you doubting your ability within hours. It can paralyze the ability of a confident business executive that usually wakes up in the morning excited and full of energy. It can confuse a leader at the top of their chosen profession or weigh down a businessperson until they're lost in a fully manifested forest of negative thoughts.

Tragically this jungle can render you totally incapacitated. You lose the ability to develop your business in a positive proactive manner. Sadly this is the fate of too many highly motivated, highly educated business people. Folks with big dreams can throw all the energy and passion they can muster at their day and still can get lost in this forest. Their heads are full of negative thoughts. Things that were mistakes have now grown into catastrophes. They were items of concern for sure but they have grown out of proportion. They live up to the saying, **"Don't make a mountain out of a molehill!"**

If you are nodding your head because you connect with this chapter, you've probably made the mistake of letting a molehill turn into a mountain. Mistakes and problems are part of life. The chance of having an awesome day, every day, where everything goes your way is highly unlikely. So greet obstacles as they appear and work the problem at hand. Too much negative up stairs isn't good. Sometimes we need a check up from the neck up so we can see clearly and solve problems while they are still molehills.

Maybe you're an athlete; you could be a professional or a weekend warrior, it doesn't matter. If you make a bad play with the puck or ball, focusing on that mistake will take your mind in a negative direction. You'll mess up the next play too. Again, don't let that molehill grow into a mountain. Of course you need to learn from your mistakes, however gripping the stick or bat too tightly takes away your skill. If you have thoughts of pervious mistakes flowing through your head, gaining their own identity you become cautious and hesitant, stifling your own natural abilities the ability to operate as a top athlete or businessperson.

Nothing is exempt from this principle. Something is always expanding in our minds. We can choose to expand on the positive things happening for us. We can choose to focus on the knowledge and skills we possess. But to do this we must discipline ourselves to keep the negative thoughts at bay. If we focus on working the problems at hand we can **"fail forward"** by learning from our mistakes, moving on, and celebrating what we have learned. I'm sure you have heard the saying **"he or she is a glass half full or a glass half empty kind of guy or gal."** Folks that let go of their mistakes quickly are glass half full people, folks that hold onto negative thoughts **"make mountains out of molehills"** are glass half empty people.

You might be wondering what this all has to do with this chapters title, **"The Cows are Out."** Well you see cows are interesting animals and they have been known to escape. When a 1,500 pound animal leans on a fence, sometimes the fence falls over. The cows then see an opportunity to explore some new ground, so off they go on their adventure. (Maybe they're looking for greener grass too.) The thing is… cows don't run away. It's not like one farmer says to another, "Hey I lost a few cows. They're about 1,500 pounds, black and white, have you seen any like that?" This conversation never happens because cows don't run away, that's not what they do. What they do is find the closest road and stand on it. Breaching the fence, manoeuvring through the ditch, eating a little green grass, and climbing up onto the road is a complete adventure. It's almost as if they just wait there to see how long it takes the farmer to notice them. Once the farmer sees that his cows are currently enjoying a newly found freedom, he just goes out rounds them up and back through the breached fence they go. It's really not that complicated. The cows really don't want to go anywhere they're happy on the farm. The whole process for the farmer is not that dramatic. For the farmer, the cows can even become a useful excuse. If the farmer doesn't want to attend an event or if he or she is a little late all that is needed is a quick apology and the knowledge that the cows were out. I mean it's hard to argue with that, it's not like you can leave them standing on the road. So Dad I forgive you for being late for my wedding… I know the cows were out.

The point I'm making here is on the farm the cows get out on a regular basis and it's not that big of a deal. The farmer just rounds them up and repairs the hole in the fence where they escaped. Overall the cows are pretty cooperative.

If the farmer replaced all his fences on the farm every time the cows got out, well, that would be quite the overreaction.

The principle is quite simple. Hey you made a mistake. I get it. It happens to everyone. OK the cows are out, put them back in and move along. Beating yourself up because the cows of your life got out can inflict massive damage to your mindset. Just let those negative thoughts in and molehills turn into mountains and suddenly you're lost in a jungle of negativity. Don't create unnecessary obstacles. Life can be tough… don't let your imagination make it tougher.

As a business coach I talk to folks on a weekly basis. When we discuss their previous week I hear a lot about their mistakes. They say, "Well Rob, last week I screwed this up, or I made this mistake, or I was supposed to do this and I didn't and I feel sick about it." By the time we have this discussion they've been dwelling on this issue for days. It's not uncommon for a client to be so engulfed by this situation that they even consider leaving their job. Their mistake has expanded to gigantic proportions.

So folks from now on go easy on yourself. When the cows of life get out, don't panic, just put them back in mend the fence and move along. When you make a mistake or things don't go your way get used to saying. *"THE COWS ARE OUT!"* Round them up then get on with your awesome life. **Something is always expanding in your mind!**

In a nutshell

We all make mistakes everyone does, whether we did something we know we should not have done or we didn't do something that we know we should have. Either way the cows are out let's round them up fix the fence and move along. If the farmer replaced all his fences on the farm because the cows escaped that would qualify as a massive over reaction on the farmers behalf, so when you make a mistake don't make that same error. Don't make a mountain out of a mole hill. Mend the fence move along.

Helpful Exercise #5

We've all made mistakes, we all have a few things that we need to forgive ourselves for, and move on. Below write down three things that you need to let go. Three things that you need to say, " You're gone. Enough of you. You're out of here!" You start the point and I'll finish it for you.

You're gone #1

_____

you're gone!

You're gone #2

_____

you're gone!

You're gone #3

_____

you're gone!

Holding on to negative feelings hurts everyone!

49

When you wake up every day
you have two choices.
You can either be positive or negative;
an optimist or a pessimist.
I choose to be an optimist.
It's all a matter of perspective.

Harvey Mackay

Six

Burn the Boats

The saying, **"burn the boats,"** is credited to Hernando Cortez. The story goes this way. Cortez arrives from Cuba to Mexico. His plan is quite simple. He wants to conquer the country and reap its riches. So in the spring of 1519 Cortez arrives on the shores of the Yucatan peninsula, with eleven ships, and six hundred and thirty men. Thirty of the men had crossbows. That's not a huge force for an invasion so Cortez needed to make a point. So apparently, he gave the order to burn the boats. To this day there's still a debate as to whether or not the order was given or if this is nothing more than a cool story with amazing applications.

I guess all those years ago there wasn't much to do… no hockey, no baseball, no watching your favourite shows at the end of a long day. There were no computers, no smart phones, none of those amazing devices that keep us in touch with life. No new gizmos, no modern sports, no internet… no wonder people spent so much time invading each other!

So back to the whole invading thing, the object was to instil as much fear as you could in your opponent. Today it's easy whoever has the biggest planes, bombs, or tanks has the advantage. You can see the difference. However years ago it was just large men with spears, swords, and bows. So I would imagine that the armies would kind of look the same, a bunch of large guys with sharp objects.

To be feared you had to do something different either something dramatic or have a reputation of doing something particularly cruel to your opponent, something that would instil fear. Which brings me back to the title of this chapter, **"Burn the Boats."** So when Cortez landed with his army of 630 large guys with sharp objects and ordered the boats to be burned, he was sending a very clear message to his opponents.

Picture it. Cortez has landed on the beach, unloaded the boats and set them aflame. What message does he want to send to the other army? They're probably watching from a ridge about a mile away. They're strategizing amongst themselves. In my mind's eye I can see one Mexican General saying to the other, "Well it looks like they have about 600 men with a decent amount of crossbowmen. We have about the same number, maybe more. So OK, it looks kind of even. We can drive them back off the beach. We have the upper ground. That could be an advantage. Oh wait! They're burning their boats. I guess these guys aren't retreating!" The message sent by Cortez was quite clear. We mean business. We do not have a plan "B". Our intentions are to conquer you and it's about to happen right now.

The point of this book is "**the grass is greener on this side of the fence**" so you might be asking why am I talking about stepping out and conquering something? Well I do want you to be content with **WHO** you are, not necessarily **WHERE** you are. As previously mentioned, I feel everyone should do their best in every aspect of their life. Which will require some intestinal fortitude to overcome obstacles and move past them. You have things to conquer. I want you to realize that you are awesome in every way, so that you can move forward. This book isn't about realizing that the grass is greener on this side of the fence so you can just put your feet up and enjoy the view. It's about accepting that your life is amazing right now, so that you have the confidence energy and aspiration to accomplish all your heart's desires wherever that takes you.

The question you should be asking yourself right now is, "Where do I need to burn the boats in my life?" What needs to be accomplished first, so I can free myself up to go out and conquer something important? It's interesting how many times I hear folks tell me they're going to try something. The word in that statement that makes me nervous is the word "try." I'd rather hear them tell me what they're going to "do." As soon as I hear the word try, I know they're already thinking about moving to plan B. The words we choose are a clear indicator of our commitment in regard to the quest at hand. When we say I'm going to try something, the boats are definitely not on fire. If Cortez was going to try to invade the Yucatan shore... he would have given the order for some of the men to stay close to the boats in case a quick escape was necessary. In this scenario, the leaders of the defending army would glance at each other with confidence because the guys on the beach looked frightened. If you really want to get somewhere, really accomplish something in your life you **must** let go of plan "B" take the plunge and make a commitment to **"burn the boats"**.

As previously mentioned, we become what we think about, not what we should be thinking about. Once you accept the fact that your life is amazing and that the grass is truly very green on this side of the fence, you're now free to climb over the fence and explore all of life's possibilities. However if your mind is constantly thinking about plan "B" that will likely be the end result. In order for plan "A" to be your destination you must spend all your energy and resources focussing on plan "A." You must eliminate all thoughts about plan "B." You must set plan "B" on fire and burn that boat. If you cut off any possibility of retreat you have a far greater chance of sticking it out through thick and thin and accomplishing plan "A." If you don't you will constantly be thinking about plan "B" and of course the concept you become what you think about will win every time. If you're wondering why this process is so challenging for people it's really quite simple, plan "B" is inside your comfort zone and plan "A" is outside. It's really that simple. A great quote on this topic is **"Everything I want is on the other side of fear. *~ Jack Canfield*"**

There are several life lessons hidden within this illustration of Cortez giving that order to burn the boats. So on your next quest, when you really want to go for something… remember what you learned from Cortez.

Life lesson #1: *Actions speak louder than words.*

As you are reading this you may be thinking that you have been talking about doing something for quite some time. The question I would like to ask you is, "When?" When are you going stop talking about it and start doing it? A little more doing and a lot less thinking would be helpful.

Life lesson #2: *You must have confidence.*

Cortez had confidence. I'm not sure all his men felt the same way at the start, but I'm sure their confidence level grew as they drew strength from their leader. If you don't feel you have the necessary confidence required **"fake it till you make it."** Show confidence on the outside and move forward. Your body will follow. You have to start somewhere. If you're trembling on the inside keep it there and show courage.

Life Lesson #3: *If you go down, go down swinging.*

In life you'll always win if you do your very best. No one is looking for better than your best. I hope you're not expecting better than your best from yourself. It's OK to strive for excellence, but expecting perfection from yourself is a disappointment waiting to happen. Of course spending most of your day pondering plan "B" if plan "A" doesn't work out, that's certainly not your best. That would be like Cortez instructing them to stay close to the boats. Will everybody always be successful at everything? Of course not but if you go down, go down swinging… not pondering plan "B"

Quite honestly folks if you want to accomplish something, anything really, large or small; allowing plan "B" to be a part of the equation is a recipe for failure. It's better to set the boats ablaze!

In a nutshell
We've all been in Cortez's shoes, metaphorically of course. Finding ourselves pushing the envelope once again, venturing outside our sacred comfort zone, into the great unknown. The easy thing of course is to stay in the safety of our comfort zone and dream about the awesome things that await us outside. It's harder to step outside and set out to chase our dreams. Once outside that cozy comfort zone the best action would be to set it ablaze immediately to eliminate any option of retreat.

Helpful Exercise #6

We all have areas of our lives that we should eliminate the possibility of retreating to plan "B". If we take away our escape route we can focus squarely at our ultimate goal. Identifying these key areas is the first step to eliminating them from our lives. Burn the boats!

Three areas in my life that I need to set ablaze are:

Burn the boat #1

_____

_____

Burn the boat #2

_____

_____

Burn the boat #3

_____

_____

Set it ablaze. Watch it burn. Move on.

Be unstoppable.

Be a force of nature.

Be fierce,

focus on your goals

and don't stop until you have succeeded.

Unknown

Seven

It's Lonely at the Bottom

There's a popular saying, **"It's lonely at the top."** I suppose life can be lonely there. I'm sure there's no shortage of executives and entrepreneurs that have gained everything and lost everything all at the same time. I'm sure lots of people have put acquiring of assets ahead of family, relationships, and values. Maybe the lure of success was so much of a temptation for them that they thought the ends justified their means of getting there. Perhaps they attended a seminar where the speaker encouraged them to reach for success without worrying about the price. I know I've heard speakers try and sell that message. Maybe it's lonely at the top because many people who get there have stepped on or ignored others as they climbed up.

I know some of these lonely people. Folks that couldn't quite seem to strike that right balance between achieving at the highest level and at the same time paying attention to the most important things in their lives. It's tricky finding that perfect balance.

I'm sure you have heard that old saying, "**You can't have your cake and eat it too.**" I have often wondered what that really means. I have never ordered cake and not eaten it and I'm quite sure that in the future when someone puts cake in front of me I will definitely eat it. Of all the quotes you can roll around in your head this one is the worst. It's not inspirational at all... I think it's a de-motivational quote. Cake is motivational. Imagine believing that two great things in a row can't go your way! That's insane. If someone puts a nice piece of cheesecake in front of you, that's great thing number one. Great thing number two is enjoying every scrumptious bite! Why can't that happen? You can absolutely have your cake and eat it too. In an abundant world, there's always more cake to find.

Don't get me wrong I certainly believe that every businessman and businesswoman should strive to be their absolute best, to operate at a level only attained by a few. I own a Real Estate coaching and training company, we push and prod our clients; we continually challenge them to get the most out of every day. I constantly remind them that each day is a gift that shouldn't be wasted. A wasted day is gone forever. Therefore, I believe we should do our absolute best to not waste days. I want our clients to have it all. I want them to balance an exhilarating business, and healthy relationships with physical and spiritual wellbeing. I have sat in many seminars and heard the speaker say you can't be a high achiever and have balance in your life; it's just not possible. I disagree. I believe they're saying that because they haven't found a way to achieve that elusive balance. Don't listen to anyone that says you have to give up happiness to succeed in business.

You can have your cake and eat it too. Not only is it possible it's actually kind of easy, I mean you have to want it. It will require a strong desire to have that amazing business, and passion to have vibrant relationships, and a commitment of time to achieve optimal physical conditioning, and a peaceful center to keep an eye on the importance of your spiritual position with the creator. It has to be your "A" plan. You've got to go for it. Achieving balance in your life must be something that's non-negotiable.

If all you can think about all day long is achieving an award or being on stage and having a superior hand you a plaque, you will never achieve balance. If that's your total focus then I guess that's what you will get. At the end of the day, there's no escaping the reality that you become what you think about. This sounds a lot like success at all cost. If you think about your business goals all day long and don't let any other thoughts in that shows what is important to you. You become what you think about. Why not use the power of your brain. It's ridiculously powerful. Focus intently on your business goals for sure, but there is also easily time in the day to focus on your relationship goals, your family goals, your health & fitness goals, and your spiritual goals. Why not have a burning desire in your spirit for multiple aspects of your life.

The truth of the matter is the vast majority of people have never really taken the time to decide what they want in life. If you're a businessman or businesswoman thinking that you want more sales, the goal is too vague. It needs to be specific. Once it's specific. "I want to increase my sales by 10% in this quarter", now if you apply ample focus, the goal creates a life of its own. The same principle applies to the other equities of your life. You have to decide exactly what you want … not kind of what you want… exactly what you want. "I want to see 80% of my children's soccer games this season." Just keep going. What kinds of relationships do you want? "I want a date night with my spouse once a week." What would that mature spiritual position look like to you? What physical fitness goals would you like to set? You don't necessarily need to become a personal trainer, maybe you just want to feel comfortable in a bathing suit. That way you can prefer summer over winter and when friends ask you to go to the beach you won't have to make up an excuse. If your focus is only on your business aspirations, if that's your all-consuming focus then that's the only set of goals you'll achieve. It will be difficult, if not impossible, to keep some of the other things around you that you should be cherishing.

So I suppose the saying, "**it's lonely at the top,**" is quite true, unfortunate but true. Imagine having every business success on one hand and nothing on the other hand. That would be like having your cake but not being able to eat it. This situation is a result of a success at all cost mindset that focussing on one thing and one thing only, is the path to a successful career. From the outside, this person would be sitting pretty. It would appear that they had everything that money could buy. Most folks would trade places with this person if they could. But once they made the trade and lived it for a few weeks they might want to trade back. The appearance of an amazing life can come with a hollow feeling of despair, hence the saying it's lonely at the top. It's sad to say a lot of folks live these exact lives; it's a shame really. It's kind of sad to have everything and be so lonely all at the same time, especially when the solution is so simple. Set goals for your business, relationships, physical condition and your spiritual position. Think about them nonstop every day. Use every ounce of energy you can muster up and watch all the important things grow a life of their own. Imagine having it all… really having it all. Decide exactly what you want in every aspect of your life and don't let go under any circumstances.

Although everything written so far is true, it certainly can be lonely at the top, unnecessary but true. "**Lonely at the bottom,**" is even a bigger tragedy. At the top, at least you have possessions, money and the means to get around. At the bottom you've got nothing. That's where it would really be lonely. This is where you could feel trapped or even desperate. This is a situation everyone on the planet should take all available measures to avoid. The temptation here is to ignore all the equities of your life and focus only on business with the belief that you will fix the others when the financial dilemma is solved. This leaves you isolated. Without a focus on family, friends, fitness, and spiritual wellbeing you are unnecessarily vulnerable to the ups and downs of the business world. Those extras don't weigh you down; they buoy you up. They make you more resilient. So I have some good news, this situation is easier to fix than you might imagine. First as previously mentioned decide what you want and then with unrelenting commitment spend all your waking hours focusing on the specific goals you have set in each important area of your life. I'm here to tell you that I've been there, and that you can do it just like so many others. Miraculously you will begin to notice change almost immediately after your journey has begun.

Sometimes life seems to throw us some curve balls, no one is exempt from this. Of course, you are more resistant or durable if you have a stronger balance in your life. Sometimes perspective has a lot to do with this. The way we perceive things spins them differently in our minds. An excellent story to illustrate this point goes like this. There is a store where you can take the cross that you're bearing and switch it for a different cross of less burden a man takes the cross he is bearing into the store where he can trade the cross for another cross, he looks around at all the crosses and notices a small one over in the corner. He picks it up and examines it. His thought is, this would make the burden much easier to manage. So into his pocket it goes. As he is leaving, the shop owner inquires about the cross. The man says, "I'm switching for this little cross which will be a lot easier for me." The shop owner informs him that he cannot leave with that particular cross. When the man, a little puzzled, inquires as to why… the shop owner informs him that it was the cross he brought in! Once we look at everyone else's burdens our own don't look so hard to manage.

Is it lonely at the top? It can be. Lonely at the bottom is a much bigger issue. Figure out what's really important to you. Set the wider goals required, focus nonstop, and watch the magic happen.

In a nutshell
Is it lonely at the top? I guess it is for some folks. Sacrificing so many aspects of their lives for business success can give the appearance of having it all on the outside and leave hollowness on the inside. Is this a mistake? Of course it is! However nothing compares to being lonely at the bottom; it's the bigger of the two tragedies. At least at the top you possess things, not that true happiness can be found in things, but if you are going to be lonely you might as well have the comforts of life. The right plan would be to set goals in ALL the important areas of your life and use your incredible brain to focus on them. It's an abundant world. You can have success in more than one area of your life. You can have your cake and eat it to!

Helpful Exercise #7

You can have your cake and eat it to. The world is an abundant place. There's enough cake to go around. You have the power and the control to set goals in multiple areas of your life. Great things can happen in more than one place at a time. You just have to decide what you want and commit to it. Once you identify what's important, you can set goals in each area of your life and focus on them. What do you want to have happen this year?

Spiritual Goal

_____

_____

_____

Family Goal

_____

_____

_____

Physical Goal

_____

_____

_____

Relationships Goal

_____

_____

_____

Business Goal

_____

_____

_____

In my opinion and in my life
this is the order of importance.

Talent is God given,
be humble.

Fame is man given,
be grateful.

Conceit is self-given
be careful.

John Wooden

Eight

Make Them Proud

For most of us, our families immigrated to North America a few generations ago. Some of you folks are first generation North Americans, probably following the path of previous family members. Even the Native American people travelled to this land long ago as people spread out around the globe.

It's a difficult decision to leave everything behind and move to a new country in the hopes of building a better life. As the offspring of immigrants we are duty bound to repay our ancestors by making them proud. If you really reflect on the magnitude of their decision, it was quite the undertaking. They decided to leave everything they were familiar with behind. They embarked on an adventure in a new country half way around the world. It was a new and developing country, not the North America we know today. It was a fledgling country of trees, mountains and pristine lakes; a rugged place that was not easily tamed. Our ancestors were the work force that built both Canada and the United States of America.

These folks started a process, a process that they would never see completed. There's a Greek proverb that says, **"A society grows great when old men plant trees whose shade they know they shall never sit in."** This process is still moving forward. Our ancestors, men and women, were the courageous people that put this great endeavour in motion. These folks said good-bye to family, friends, church groups, co-workers, and a familiar way of life that supported their family tree for thousands of years. They sold everything, boarded a boat and with mixed emotions watched their homeland fade over the horizon. As they journeyed across the ocean, typically a ten-day voyage, I wonder how much reassuring was taking place to offset the excitement and anticipation of a new beginning. There must have been a feeling of loss in the reality that they would probably never see their homeland again or any of the people they left behind. I would imagine there would be a whole lot of "things are going to be fine" mutterings in unsure tones and probably a healthy dose of "what the heck have we done" conversations as well.

I wonder how they felt upon arrival, as they saw the East coast rising from the horizon and taking form. As they viewed their new home for the first time; a land they had been thinking about for quite a while. A beautiful land for sure, and definitely a land of progress that offered an opportunity for them to play an important role. As they stepped onto new soil you can imagine them wondering, "What now?" When we travel today we are whisked away to a swanky resort or picked up at the airport for a quick ride home. We go home to familiar surroundings, home to sleep in our comfortable and familiar beds. Not for these folks. They stood on the pier with their luggage and looked at each other. North America wasn't home yet.

Our ancestors spent their working lives building the infrastructure you and I see today. They brought the flavour of the old world with them by creating small communities within the larger social fabric where they could share their culture. They made homes away from their homeland and mingled new traditions with old.

So the question is why would they do this? Why would they take this huge risk and face the danger of heading into the great unknown? I'm sure they had heard from others that had gone ahead of them of the prospects in this new untapped land… **the land of opportunity.** That would have been reassuring to them. I'm quite sure they pinned their hopes on that. However, they didn't know it for sure, they hadn't experienced it yet. It was just a dream, a belief that things would work out.

I would imagine that some people took the risk believing there would be a better life for them personally. Others were fleeing political or religious persecution or famine. For these individuals, the prospect of staying in their home country was just not an option. Leaving was a chance to get somewhere safe. They were looking for a place that would accept their personal beliefs; where they were free to live the way they wanted. But, I think for the majority of people the greatest reason to move was the benefit it would provide for their children and their children's children. Many parents gave up their established livelihood to face the challenges of learning a new language and working in menial jobs so that their children would have greater opportunities and greater freedoms. It was a huge sacrifice on their part to give future generations a better chance to succeed. They made a decision to sacrifice for the greater good. They made a commitment to be the people that would put things in motion so others would benefit. I wonder what they thought and talked about in the first few years, while things were taking shape. I wonder how much they encouraged and motived each other to keep going... to keep moving in a positive direction.

As previously mentioned, many of these courageous settlers never returned to their homeland, they left family members who they never saw again and when they said goodbye it meant forever. Now it's possible to take a quick flight back to our homeland and check out our heritage. We can visit the city, town, or village where our ancestors lived and make emotional connections to help us better understand our roots. Those that immigrated after World War II probably have returned to their homeland to visit and to show their children the land from which they came. However for those that immigrated in the early 1900's, the 1800's or even earlier there was probably no chance to return. It simply wasn't as easy or safe as it is today. After all they were busy working hard to create the awesome situation we enjoy today. That's what was important to them, that's what they came for and that's what they spent their time doing, building an awesome future for us.

Statistically North America is the most opportunistic environment ever known to mankind. If you have the ambition to make something of yourself there has never been a better time or place to reach for success. That's the situation and the environment that our fore fathers and mothers built for us. That was their plan and they executed it perfectly. They sacrificed what was important to them and built an awesome future for us. It's their long hours, blood, sweat and sacrifice that created this opportunity for us today. I mentioned earlier that we owe it to them to honour their sacrifice. We do that by taking advantage of all the opportunities they afforded us. They did what they did so we can have the opportunities that we have.

Can you imagine an immigrant couple making a decision about a hundred years ago to forgo everything, immigrate to North America, to be part of the great undertaking? What would they think if they knew their seventeen year-old great, great grandson has dropped out of school and joined a street gang? This young person is being disrespectable to his ancestors. Of course his great, great grandparents would have no way of knowing this, but if they could I'm sure they would say, "That's not why we made the sacrifice."

You might be thinking, I'm not in a gang. I'm a law-abiding citizen! True. However are you being all you can be? Are you doing your very best? Are you taking advantage of the sacrifices your ancestors made to give you the opportunities set before you? Are you honouring their sacrifice? Are you leaving the world a better place for the generations that follow? If your great, great grandparents could watch you, would they say, "OK that makes our sacrifice worthwhile? We're glad to see how well you're doing and how much you're enjoying the great nation we created for you. We're enjoying watching you contribute to society and help others. You're making a positive difference. We're glad you are our legacy." Would they be that impressed? Would they be proud that their family name still stood strong and upright and feel they had made the right call getting on the boat all those years ago? Or would they say, "Wow we gave all we had, we did all we could do and this is the result! Our offspring don't appear to be happy. They're not leaders in their fields and they don't seem to have that get up and go attitude that we had. Something seems to have been lost along the way. If we had known it would turn out like this maybe we should just have stayed home, lived our lives and not made the sacrifice."

What would your ancestors say? Too many people go through life and never seem to connect with that inner energy that inner commitment that their fore fathers and mothers were able to grab hold of and exercise the discipline to not let go of under any circumstances. They don't have the ability to focus on the finish line and run through it at top speed to complete the race.

The good news is it's not too late; it's never too late. You can start to make your ancestors proud now. You can begin to make changes, to take advantage of the opportunities that were created for you on purpose. You're not a tree you can move. You're not stuck in one place. You can move around and make decisions that will take you in the right direction. Look for what has you stuck in a rut and change it. By the way, you know you are in a rut in life when you wake up in the morning and plan your nap! Think about it. Waking up at 6:00 AM on a workday, laying in bed while you shake out the cobwebs. Mentally running through your day…."OK. I need to go here and there. I need to pick up this and that. And then I can have a nap." When you plan your nap before you get out of bed that's a sure sign you are in a rut! This isn't what your ancestors had in mind when they set up this country for you. *"You don't have to go from zero to hero."* Just get out of bed and start moving in the right direction. Set some small goals and start working toward them, get in the habit of accomplishing things.

If reading this chapter puts a little pressure on you to live a life that would honour your ancestors, that's a good thing and a good start. They made a huge sacrifice for us; we shouldn't let them down. We should **make them proud**! The reality that they created for us is so amazing and so precious that hundreds of thousands of young men and women have given their lives to protect the countries that those nervous settlers played a part in creating. I'm talking about my ancestors and your ancestors, people that we are forever indebted to. They came here and they made their lives count. I highly recommend you do the same.

In a nutshell

We have a responsibility to honour those that went before us and created the opportunities that are waiting for us… right here, right now. The possibilities are endless. We have arrived at a perfect time. Our ancestors have created and defended this land of opportunity. This wasn't an easy task. We owe them our respect. We need to live up to their contributions; to continue their legacy. This hasn't all happened, so that you and I could just float through life and not make our mark. That would be simply unacceptable.

Helpful Exercise #8

Although it's Ok to enjoy the luxuries and benefits of life, we need to remember the sacrifices made for us in order for us to truly appreciate all of life's pleasures. It's important that we add to what's been built for us. We're here for a reason there's work to be done. We need to leave behind a positive legacy of our own. Write down a contribution you have made that would make your ancestors proud and one you are working on now. Identify something you would like to contribute in the future and what you would like your great, great grandchildren to recognize as your legacy.

A contribution I have made is:

_____

_____

A contribution I am working on is:

_____

_____

A contribution I would like to make in the future is:

_____

_____

I want my legacy to be:

_____

_____

We all have a part to play. What's your part?

You cannot escape the responsibility of tomorrow by evading it today

Abraham Lincoln

Nine

The Scarecrow

I can say for sure that, *"a scarecrow has never harmed a crow."* Obviously we know that would be impossible, scarecrows are not real. However think about it from the crow's perspective. That scarecrow is a very scary dude. It creates a real and bona fide situation. The interesting thing about this circumstance is that, everywhere there's a scarecrow there's a vegetable patch or a cornfield, exactly the nourishment the crow needs. Everywhere a scarecrow is erected, is exactly the place a crow wants to be. For a crow, a scarecrow should be like the giant sign advertising a mall. When we're travelling and we need something, those huge signs tell us how to find the mall parking lot and we're good to go! It should be the same for crows. If they're flying into new territory with an unknown landscape just find a scarecrow and you found lunch

Imagine two crows travelling together one saying to the other, "That looks good down there, we should check it out." The other crow would reply, "Do you see a scarecrow? Those are the best places! If there are two it's probably a buffet."

Of course this isn't the way it goes. Crows don't fly around looking for scarecrows; in fact they avoid them. To a crow, a scarecrow means danger, imagined danger for sure, but nevertheless danger in the mind of that crow. That's what's interesting about fear. Real fear, the mortal danger type and imagined fear, where no real danger is present, are indistinguishable in our minds. They both give that gripping, paralyzing panic-like reaction to our bodies. Our hearts begin to thump and we feel that adrenaline rush. There are dangerous situations in real life. Perhaps your boat capsizes and there are great white sharks circling. Or maybe you're lost in the jungle where everything is either hunting or being hunted. You can insert the real world scenario here that holds your greatest personal fear... When we're in potentially harmful situations our brain releases chemicals into our blood stream to assist us, as our brain makes the transition to survival mode.

One of the interesting things about the brain is that it doesn't differentiate between real danger and imagined danger. So if you did unfortunately find yourself in that real danger situation where you are lost in the jungle, or your boat capsized in shark infested waters you would be happy your body was getting you ready to fight or for flight. These dangers feel very real and are very real.

However…. we get the same kind of adrenaline rush from the special effects in a movie. Think how many people saw the movie JAWS and were scared out of the water. Imagined fear provides a danger scenario where there really isn't an opportunity for personal harm but it feels like there is. The brain in this situation releases those same chemicals into your body that same survival mode clicks in. There isn't any real danger but your mind tells you there is.

Think about the crows; the scarecrow has fooled them ever since the dawn of time, right from the time man has planted crops. You may say to yourself, "Silly crows, not the sharpest tools in the shed." But, before you're too hard on the crows you might want to take a look at your own life. Take a look at where you have erected some scarecrows, some areas you are avoiding. Are there some places that would be beneficial to visit but your mind says, "Danger." I'm not talking about visiting the wrong side of the tracks; I'm talking about places where the danger exists only in your mind.

Seeing as I'm a business coach, please allow me to use some business illustrations. You may not be in sales, but I'm sure you can simply transfer the scarecrow in the story to another vegetable patch that better suits your personal situation. Perhaps you've been asked to give a speech or present at the office sales meeting. Maybe you've been given the opportunity to be the Master of Ceremonies at a special occasion. There's no real danger present in these situations. They represent an awesome opportunity for some personal growth. This is one of those places where only imagined dangers lurk. There are no sharks in the room, at least not real ones, just perhaps some metaphorical ones. It's interesting that the fear of public speaking can be so overwhelming that many people would probably pass on this personal growth opportunity. Unfortunately speaking in public and the other opportunities may currently reside outside your comfort zone. The thought of engaging something or someone that resides on the other side of your comfort zone sends a shockwave through your body, and encourages you to pull back. Maybe it's something as simple as a sales person trying to muster up the courage to make prospecting calls. The comedian, Jonathan Winters said, **"If your ship doesn't come in, swim out to it."** In sales he's right. Those calls are important, but if they provoke a fear response they are likely to go unmade. Even if there is no real danger and no real need to be frightened. All of us can think of our own imaginary fears that hold us back.

In these cases the imagined fear seems very threatening. It feels every bit as real as the mortal danger fear. It feels the same but it's definitely not the same, one has danger and the other does not. That fact makes them significantly different, even though your body is overcome with emotion, it's important to understand that they're not the same. We should obviously avoid situations with mortal danger fear, However, we need to visit and wrestle with the imagined fear, the scarecrow, to stretch our comfort zone. I like to think of the following acronym:

F – alse
E – vidence
A – ppearing
R – eal

The fear feels real, which of course makes it real in your mind even though it is devoid of mortal danger. It's just something outside your comfort zone, something you have yet to bring inside the circle, something that you don't yet fully understand.

If you really think about it, imagined fear has its own negative consequence. It's not as bad as having your boat capsize with fins on the horizon or being lost in a jungle with big squeezy snakes. But imagined danger can hold you with the same gripping even paralyzing fear. It can shut you down, render you in incapacitated and inhibit your ability to move forward, and grow as an individual. It can stand in your way and hinder the process of expanding your comfort zone.

Think about the relationship a crow has with a scarecrow. It sounds silly to us that a couple of sticks, a straw hat, and some hay would be a sufficient deterrent to protect the farmers precious crop, from those pesky crows. I wonder if the crows watch and think that the silly humans being frightened off by their own imaginary scarecrows.

Think about what would happen if the crows were smart enough to expand their comfort zone to include scarecrows. They would fly around looking for scarecrows! What an easy way to find everything you need to survive. The scarecrows might as well be holding signs saying, **"Live the good life."**

If we're honest with ourselves we would see that we've often erected scarecrows exactly where we need to go. The scarecrows in our personal lives represent the False Evidence Appearing Real scenario. When we are asked to do something, or we know we need to or would like to do something, but this item or person is outside our comfort zone we hesitate. It's scary. We put up our defences even though nothing is attacking.

If you want to identify what's holding you back; take a moment and ask yourself a few questions;

Where have I erected scarecrows?

Are these fears real?

Is there any mortal danger?

Is this fear just in my mind?

Is this a False Evidence Appearing Real situation, or am I in some mortal danger? Is the danger real or just perceived as real? They may feel the same but you need to be able to call them by name. You want to treat them differently.

The scarecrows in our lives are only there because we put them there. They didn't erect themselves. They don't have a mind of their own. Remember, they're not real. I know they feel real but at the end of the day they're not real. They consist of nothing more than a few sticks, some old clothes and a scary hat. That's it. You put them there and you can just as easily take them down, move forward and accomplish all you are capable of with this precious time you've been given.

Don't be a silly crow that wastes an entire life being frightened away by something that isn't even real. Crows spend all that extra time searching for sustenance, when all they need to do is look for scarecrows and have abundance in their lives. Crows make their circumstances even more devastating by teaching their offspring to avoid the scarecrows, guiding a whole new generation to search for food, to carve out an existence all the while avoiding life's easy path.

Ask yourself honestly, where have I accidently erected scarecrows? The more scarecrows you have the smaller your comfort zone will be. I've met folks with so many scarecrows active in their daily lives they really can't do anything. They are stuck. Stuck in life with little chance of getting where they want to go. Think about it, a crow is flying around looking for some food. All he sees are dozens of scarecrows, so he just keeps on flying on searching and searching.

If only the crow could see past the **False Evidence Appearing Real**, life would be so much easier. Life can be hard, but it definitely doesn't need to be this way. If you can recognize the scarecrows in you life you can take them down. Maybe for you it's just a case of speaking up and talking to people **"scarecrow"** telling a joke at a party **"scarecrow"** Speaking your mind **"scarecrow"** speaking in public **"scarecrow"** and so on. In many cases we have put up scarecrows in places to avoid embarrassment. That's not a good enough reason to justify living our lives in a small box. A comfort zone that fits too tightly isn't useful. It's better to have a comfort zone that is large enough to let us grow and explore.

If I were a crow advisor, instead of a business advisor, I would tell them to locate a new scarecrow every day and enjoy all of the benefits that come with conquering that false fear. We should give ourselves that advice. Eleanor Roosevelt suggested people should, **"Do one thing every day that scares you."** Every day we should seek out a place where we have inadvertently placed a scarecrow. One thing I can guarantee for sure is, if you installed a scarecrow, there is something there for you.

For the crow, everything they want is on the other side of fear. The same applies to you.

In a nut shell

A scarecrow has never harmed a crow. We know that because scarecrows are not real. The point is, they feel real to the crows and that's all that matters. Crows see a scarecrow and stay away, even though everything they need for their sustenance is right beside the scarecrow. Unfortunately, we face the same challenge. We erect scarecrows in our lives. They feel real to us, but there not. They're as artificial as the scarecrows. But, it's sad to say that they're just as effective at keeping us from moving forward toward our goals. The grass is greener on this side of the fence, let's eliminate all our scarecrows and enjoy it.

Helpful Exercise #9

Unfortunately a lot of people are faced with real danger in their lives. Their fear is not imagined. However, many more of us live lives of quiet desperation because we imagine our world is frightening. Imagined fear isn't real even though it feels real. If you're in real danger you should take the appropriate steps to distance yourself from this situation. But, if you're just behaving like a crow trying to avoid a scarecrow that's totally different; that fear is imaginary. It's holding you back and you have the power to laugh in its face. It's time to identify the scarecrows in your life!

Scarecrow #1

_____

_____

Scarecrow #2

_____

_____

Scarecrow #3

_____

_____

Just because it seems real doesn't mean it is.

Don't believe what your eyes are telling you.

All they show is limitation.

Look with your understanding,

find out what you already know,

and you will see the way to fly

Richard Bach

Ten

You Can't Put the Toothpaste Back in the Tube

I first heard the saying; **"You can't put the toothpaste back in the tube. "** many years ago when I was new to the business world. I was discussing an office problem with my broker, a wise man and an extremely successful businessperson. He quoted this saying and it struck a chord with me. There's truth in these words, "You can't put the toothpaste back in the tube." I've allowed this statement to govern my thinking ever since.

As a business coach, I hear a lot of stories from my clients. They tell me about the mistakes they've made and the things they should or shouldn't have done. I would say that I hear "for lack of a better word" confessions five maybe ten times per week. So I have no shortage of opportunities to use what I think is one of the most liberating and empowering saying, "You can't put the tooth paste back in the tube."

We all make mistakes. We all have problems. The important point is what do we do next? After the mistake is made, are you able to get your head around the fact that what is done is done. Or are you going to compound things and make the situation worse. I'm not suggesting that you shouldn't care or create a nonchalant attitude about your actions. I'm just pointing out that what's done is done. The thought that you can't put toothpaste back in the tube isn't an immature thought or position. It's quite the opposite. When something is done it's done. It's time to accept that you made a mistake and take a mature position. That puts you in a position to apologize or to forgive others and to focus on moving towards a solution.

If you have children, especially teenagers, they will do things that they shouldn't do on a regular basis. Making mistakes and pushing boundaries is an important part of growing up and finding their way in life. When they make a mistake, there's no point in trying to put the toothpaste back in the tube. It just doesn't go back in. I don't know how they put that stripped toothpaste in the tube to start with, but once it's out on the counter you might as well start looking for a solution. You might as well be a mature, solution-oriented person as opposed to a reactionary, fly-off-the handle individual that escalates the problem. Again I'm not suggesting that there won't be consequences for the mistake. One of the best lessons you can teach your kids is to accept responsibility and the natural consequences of their actions. Luckily, most of the time when an error is made it's not that big of a deal.

Every once in a while mistakes carry some significant repercussions. In either case you're better off with the mindset that, "You can't put tooth paste back in the tube." Once you admit that what's done is done and you can't undo it you're ready to move forward. This is definitely life's less travelled road but it is the easiest one to take because you can put all of your energy into making things right. I mentioned teenagers earlier, simply because they give us opportunities on a regular basis to exercise our ability to handle situations, challenges and circumstances in a mature grown up fashion. Even if we have to repeat, "I'm the adult. I'm the adult." over and over again in our minds before we respond in a cool calm fashion.

It helps you remain humble if you remember the major mistakes you've made in life. We've all made some doozies. It doesn't matter how you get tangled up in a situation, whether it's your fault or someone else's. The point is you're involved; the important thing now is are you going to be a solution-oriented person. Are you going to travel the correct road, that less travelled mature road, that solution finding road or are you going to make this current circumstance even worse. It's sad to say they call it the less travelled road for a reason; it's the road few take. Few ever understand the importance of this road.

If I could quote a scripture, James 4:14, "For what is your life? It is even a vapour, that appeareth for a little time, and then vanisheth away." In the big scheme of things we play a small part in regard to our planet. It really is a tragedy to spend so much time worrying and overreacting to life's common challenges that we forget to live. Again, I know that every once in a while life sends us a serious challenge, a challenge that can set us back and totally occupy our time until it's solved. This happens, however most of the time we get hung up on the little stuff. Everyday problems are a hassle for sure but they're not something that's going to affect your life going forward. Will a child need to be grounded? Maybe. Will a relationship need to be altered? Perhaps an adjustment is going to be necessary. That's it; an adjustment is going to be required. That's the point, just a small life adjustment and move along. Stop and ask yourself, "Will this matter 10 minutes from now? Will it matter 10 days from now? Will it matter 10 years from now?" Then act accordingly. The opposite would be to make a huge deal about everything and you're back to making mountains out of molehills. That's exactly what you're doing when something in the non-life changing group comes along and you're not able to get your head around the fact that in the big picture this situation really doesn't matter.

Life does send us some mountains every now and again that we need to climb. But it doesn't make a lot of sense to make things worse by creating our own mental mountains. So make sure you know how to spot a molehill when it comes into your life. It's just a bump along the road. Make the right choice. Choice number one would be to say; "Well I can't put the toothpaste back in the tube so I need a solution. Where do I go from here?

What is the simplest way to fix this minor problem?" Choice number two, would be to ignore the mature solution and overreact. This might involve getting angry, blaming the problem on someone else, or ignoring it in the hopes that it will go away. Make the right choice. When a molehill comes your way look for the solution right away and don't let it grow into a mountain range.

Practise on the molehills in your life because life does send us some bona fide mountains every now and again that we need to climb. The same approach is needed. "You still can't put the toothpaste back in the tube." The mountain needs to be dealt with. The process doesn't change with the magnitude of the problem. So when something really bad appears like a house fire, or a frightening medical diagnosis, or the loss of a job, accept what has happened and look for solutions. With the ebb and flow of life, situations and circumstances change. We get some mountains but mostly molehills. Sometimes we confuse the two. Look for solutions. You may be able to turn some mountains back into molehills and then eliminate them from your life.

Unfortunately, most people live their lives believing they are coping with a mountain range of problems. I'm not saying your problems are not real. I'm just not sure why you are holding onto, and nurturing them.

In a nutshell

Do we all have challenges? Yes of course we do that's called life. It's how we deal with inconveniences that seem to come our way on a regular basis that is important. Sometimes people think that the grass is greener on the other side of the fence because all they can see is a mountain of challenges on their side. The truth is many mountains appear because you've created them out of molehills. You haven't found a way to deal with them and let them go. That means that if you were to move to the other side of the fence, over time you would just collect a new mountain range. "You can't but the toothpaste back in the tube." Recognize mistakes and problems right away. What's done is done. Find a solution or make amends. Move on.

Helpful Exercise #10

It's very common for people to over react when things happen; sometimes even more over reacting follows. Which is how we make mountains out of molehills. The first step is to realize what you're doing and to stop. This is easier said than done. Take a moment to reflect on some of the situations in your life where you may be building a mountain by over reacting. Are you making the problem worse? Is it really just a molehill that you've tripped over? Acknowledging what you're doing is the start.

I am currently making a mountain out of:

_____

_____

I am currently making a mountain out of:

_____

_____

I am currently making a mountain out of:

_____

_____

The difference between a mountain and a molehill is your perspective.

Although no one can go back

and make a new start,

anyone can start now

and make a new beginning.

Carl Bard

Eleven

You Don't Have to Go From Zero to Hero

One of the big mistakes that we make as individuals is trying to go from zero to hero, trying to get from where you are to where you want to be all in one big jump. In the movies, characters often go from being a zero to being a hero in just over two hours! In real life, **"you don't have to go from zero to hero."** You just need to get on a progressive path. Actually going from zero to hero, getting from where you are right now to another place in life in a short period of time in most cases is an unrealistic expectation.

A key unlocks a door and allows you entry to what lies beyond that door. There are some keys that will unlock the pathway to your awesome future. There is a progressive path that will take you to the future you're dreaming about. That amazing future is there and available to you for sure, the trick is how do you get there? What keys will open the doors? What is the sequence of events that will get you to your desired results?

The first key is acceptance.

You have to begin where you are. You're amazing. You're unique. Accept it. You should be OK with who you are. On the other hand, you may not be OK with where you are. You may not be happy with your accomplishments to date in regard to your life status, or income, or home, or spiritual position, friends, family, health and so on. It's normal to have a desire to improve your position in life. Some would say it's your responsibility. I imagine you would agree with me that it's important to always do your best, to make your mark in life, to leave the planet a better place than you found it, and to be on that path of constant personal improvement and fulfillment.

Even though we should absolutely do our very best to reach our potential, that doesn't change the fact that we should be OK with who we are. Who we are in life and where we are in life; are two very different things, they sound similar but they're not. One is east and one is west. Unfortunately if we can't manage the task of separating these two positions, we can find ourselves not accepting **"who we are"** and that inadvertently hinders us moving forward with **"where we want to be."**

Any person that cannot find a way to be OK and accepting of themselves will have a very difficult time getting to where they want to be in life. I'm being generous by saying they would have a difficult time moving forward and achieving their dreams. The truth is it might be close to impossible. If you take a close look, your life is probably pretty cool. If you take a few minutes and write out the top ten things you love about your life and about yourself, you'll probably see that you have a lot of good things going on. The first key in **"We don't have to go from zero to hero,"** is accepting yourself as a pretty cool person. Remember you are the only person on the planet with your fingerprints and your DNA. So if you're on a quest to be special and unique that's already been accomplished

The second key is patience.

Patience is not everyone's strongest suit. It's not mine, but nevertheless it's the second key. It's difficult to be patient when you so badly want change. I know; I've certainly been there many times. I'm there now. I'm always looking to change for the better. Keep in mind you should be on a campaign to change where you are in life not who you are, I can't over state this point.

Lack of patience, being in a hurry causes errors. That leads to frustration, possible failure and potentially the abandonment of a worthwhile goal. Again, you don't have to go from zero to hero; you just need to be on a progressive path that will lead you to your ultimate desired goal. The trick is to set small goals and work on accomplishing them one at a time. There's a saying **"Inch by inch life's a cinch. Yard by yard life is hard."** So identify small manageable tasks and work on them one at a time, small bite size pieces.

When you order a nice thick juicy steak at a fine restaurant, you follow this exact principle, you cut it up into small manageable bite sized pieces and before you know it you're ordering desert. I'd even say that the process was enjoyable. Yum. Now imagine you have a twelve ounce steak sitting on your plate, you glance at the dessert tray as it passes by, hmm that dessert looks really good. You can't wait to have that. All you need to do is consume this steak and then you can have dessert. Sticking your fork into the steak and trying to eat the whole thing in one big bite isn't going to work. You won't look very dignified and people at the next table will stare. It's the same thing in life. Be patient. Cut things up into small manageable pieces and enjoy the process.

With the steak you have the enjoyment of every tasty tender piece. I realize accomplishing small tasks isn't exactly the same. It's not as delicious as eating steak. However, don't underestimate the satisfaction of conquering something small and moving to the next item. You'll find the sense of accomplishments that comes from completing a step, even a small one, does have its merits. I would recommend you write out the ten things you would like to accomplish, choose the one that you deem to be the most important and then like the steak cut it up into small manageable pieces and get started. Let's say you break the first item into six pieces then over a period of time you one by one tackle those pieces. Remember, **"You don't have to go from zero to hero."** So now you have a plan, you have your list of the ten things that you would really love to have as an active part of your life, you have selected the first item, and you broke that item into small manageable pieces. You have effectively created the plan, a plan to get from point "A" where you are to point "B" where you want to be.

The question now is do you have the self-discipline to take it one step at a time. You don't want to be impatient and try to eat the steak all in one bite. It helps to look at the positives and the negatives of being impatient. List the positives on one side and the negatives on the other. You'll probably find that the side hosting the negatives has a lot of items and the positive side would be blank. Being impatient in life only brings frustration and disappointment. Take your time. If you want to improve your position in life I would highly recommend you work on your patience.

The third key is to acknowledge accomplishment.

So you have your list and you're ready to go. Your list had ten items that were extremely important to you. You selected the item that you desire the most and made it the target of your first quest. You wrote out bite sized chunks and put them in a logical order and start eating that steak one piece at a time. You've started. Soon the first manageable piece will be history. If you have ten items and each item is broken down into six manageable pieces you are effectively 60 pieces or 60 tasks away from achieving your desired outcome. I'm suggesting that when you accomplish that first task, that first item, you should take the time to acknowledge that accomplishment. It's small and there are still 59 more adventures to come, but you've accomplished something. Celebrate. Maybe you'll just take a few minutes and reflect, or maybe you'll go out to dinner or perhaps buy a new pair of shoes. The point is the accomplishment cannot go unacknowledged. You must give yourself a pat on the back whether it is real or metaphorical. I realize the where you want to be is a long way away, that's true for sure, however you're one step closer.

There are a couple of tangible benefits in honouring small accomplishments. The first is you create anchors in your life. When you hit some rough water along the way, which is of course likely, you can look back at your accomplishments and draw some strength from them. They can give you the courage to move forward and continue to pursue your dream. The second and most important of the benefit is it just plain makes life better. Celebrating small accomplishments allows you to enjoy the process. Remember you want to make, **"the journey is as much fun is the destination."** Waiting to celebrate your accomplishment at the end of the 60 mini tasks might lead to a euphoric feeling that would be well deserved, however, wouldn't it be better to feel good all the way along. You'll still feel euphoric when it's done but now that feeling is supported by 59 smaller senses of accomplishment. That's the prescription to maximize your life.

In a nutshell

Accept **who you are**. There isn't a better you out there anywhere. **Where you are,** that's a different story. I firmly believe that we should all be on a mission to do the best we can. You should have a strong desire to leave the planet a better place than we found it. Luckily you can enjoy your quest as you go. You don't have to wait until you reach your ultimate goal to celebrate. The enjoyment of every day, the satisfaction of accomplishing small goals is the motivation that will keep you going. Do you need to get somewhere in life, somewhere important? Yes! I strongly suggest you set a series of small goals and enjoy the ride. **"You don't have to go from zero to hero."**

Helpful Exercise #11

As human beings we are not known for patience, especially in this modern instant society quick fixes for everything mindset. We do need to work on this after all Rome wasn't built in a day. If we are too impatient we miss all the little victories along the way. We also add undo stress and pressure that is in no way necessary. Where are you being impatient right now?

I'm being impatient about:

_____

_____

I'm being impatient about:

_____

_____

I'm being impatient about:

_____

_____

Things take time; breathe. You'll get there.

Trees that are slow to grow

bear the best fruit

Unknown

Twelve

The Locomotive

Some of these chapters are self explanatory and some are not. This one will take some explaining. The locomotive is about the magical world of momentum. I have the privilege of working with top business people around North America who are trying to become more productive. I start each coaching session by asking them to, **"Tell me a couple of great things that have happened since we last talked."** I want my clients to be thinking and focusing on what's working well in their businesses and personal lives; not what's not. Mindset is critical.

Imagine starting every valuable coaching session by asking the client this question, **"Ok tell me about your week."** You know we would instantly be talking about all the things that went wrong or sideways since our last conversation. It's not that we're negative people, however we seem to automatically default to the negative side for some reason. This tendency doesn't make us negative people; it just makes us normal. It seems to be what humans do. We need to make a conscious decision to automatically lean to the positive side of the ledger. We have to train our brains to think positive first. It's interesting that even though the clients know this request is coming, **"tell me a couple of great things that have happened since we last talked,"** they still often have a challenge coming up with an answer. The truth is so many awesome things have happened that they should have a problem narrowing it down to just two items or events. I should have to interrupt by saying, "Hey I have a lot to cover so let's keep it to just two amazingly unbelievable things!"

So let's get back to the idea of momentum and the connection with the locomotive. I've facilitated over 50,000 coaching sessions and started each one by requesting that people, **"tell me a couple of great things that have happened since last time we spoke."** I know everyone has two lists, a list of what's working in their life and business and a list of what's not. If we don't consciously think about it our minds usually drift to the negative list. If this habit continues unchecked, if we allow our brain to spend most of its time and energy pondering all the things that are not going our way, our life momentum is in a negative direction.

I know asking a client to, **"tell me a couple of great things that have happened since we last talked,"** is a small thing. If that was the only time that week that person thought positively; my one request wouldn't be enough to swing their mind to positive life momentum. However it's a start, it's the right principle or viewpoint. It's the correct way to spin things. First things first… what's going my way? What's the positive in this situation? How many awesome things happened to me today or this week? Count your blessings.

I'm not sure that the human brain automatically focuses on the negative because it's designed that way. Most likely it's conditioning. Our world is set up with a negative spin, when you watch the evening news it's nothing more than the three or four natural or mankind generated disasters. The evening news certainly isn't a collection of the feel good stories about what's happening on planet Earth. There are many more good things happening than bad but it's the devastating stories that seem to have more traction. No one seems to be as interested in what's working. What's not going well on our planet appears to be more engaging for the masses. Something as simple as the weather has a negative spin; you hear the weatherman or woman say Friday has a 20% chance of snow. Hey the roads will be bad on Friday it's going to snow. But, a 20% chance of snow also means there is an 80% chance it's not going to snow. It's interesting to me that they never say it that way, they never say 80% chance of no snow. It's always 20% chance of snow. This tells our brains it's going to snow on Friday. A whole host of teenagers are hoping it will snow so much that school will be cancelled and they won't have to write their math test. The truth is with this particular forecast it's probably not going to snow.

Over time with a constant bombardment of negative information it's really no surprise that our minds seem to drift to the negative. If we cannot break free from this tendency our life momentum has a negative flow. Fortunately every coin has two sides. That means we can separate ourselves from the pack and take the road less travelled. We would be in the minority for sure; we would be the ones with **positive life momentum.** When I say the road less travelled this could be more dramatic than you might think, I have no idea obviously what percentage of people have positive life momentum versus negative life momentum. It's not important what percentage is in each group, the important thing for you is to know which group you're in. If you're honest with yourself this should be obvious, you have either allowed your brain to get sucked into looking at the negative first, negative life momentum, or you look at the positive first, positive life momentum.

It's important to understand that if you see the positive first and have positive life momentum you'll have some negative thoughts and even actions. Nobody's perfect. But if you see the positive side of life most of the time you have positive life momentum. The same applies to negative thinking. If you have negative life momentum you'll still have some positive thoughts and actions. Unfortunately you see the negative first. Due to life conditioning unfortunately most folks live with negative life momentum. Think about your life. Which direction is dominant?

The good news is if you are currently in negative life momentum it's kind of easy to fix. If you have accidently allowed yourself to see the glass as half empty you're a victim of the system. Don't worry you're not alone. You're actually with the bigger crowd, but just because negative thinking is common doesn't mean it's helpful. You need to separate from the mob and become a member of the more exclusive club. So take the time to consciously look for the good in things. Begin to train your brain to see the bright side of every situation. Every cloud has a silver lining. Find it. It won't be very long until your application to the exclusive club is accepted. It's a much better way to live life; after all, **"the grass is greener on this side of the fence."**

Our lives always have momentum one way or the other. We are either experiencing positive life momentum or negative life momentum. With that in mind let's talk about the locomotive. What's the connection? What role does the locomotive play in assisting us in making the jump from the common negative life momentum to the very uncommon and exclusive positive life momentum?

If you ever watch an old western movie, you watch as the old steam locomotive fires up. It takes so much energy and so much power for that locomotive to get up and running. Steam is flying everywhere. Slowly the wheels turn over, half a turn then another half a turn, then another half a turn. There is so much steam you can hardly see the engine as it works its way up to speed. The reason so much energy is required is because when the train is at a standstill it has no momentum. Once the train is moving down the tracks all that is required is a shovel full of coal. Now the train has momentum, it takes a lot less energy to keep something going than to get it going in the first place.

If you're in sales this is an amazing metaphor to keep in mind. In sales, we need to make out-bound calls. We need to talk to people! We're in sales; that's the way it works. Whatever goods or services you sell, a certain number of people will find you every year but usually not the amount that is required to accomplish the desired goal. That's why sales people need to prospect. So think about the locomotive, if you consider that a shovel of coal is a prospecting session. All you have to do is give the locomotive engine of your business a shovel full of coal every workday. The salesperson that feeds their business engine every day has positive life momentum on their side. Things just keep rolling along.

Unfortunately most salespeople let the train come to a complete stop. They get busy with other things and stop prospecting. That deprives the locomotive of their business of that shovel full of coal every day. Unfortunately this is the exact reason why most salespeople fail. No daily coal and eventually the train grinds to a complete standstill. If you think back to that western movie you can picture all the energy required to get that locomotive up and running at top speed again.

Here's the thing it doesn't matter how many times that train stopped and started it's the same amount of energy and work to get up to speed every time. Even if the train has been in service for years it doesn't make the process any easier. It's the same for salespeople; if you let the engine of your business stop it's a huge amount of work getting it going again. People fail in sales because they exhaust themselves because they continually allow the train to stop and over time get tired of all the energy required to get it going again. So eventually they decide to pack it in. If this is your cycle you're in negative life momentum. Your locomotive keeps stopping. If you take a look at this honestly you'll see that you're actually working too hard. You can take it easier by harnessing positive life momentum. Getting the train going is still a lot of work, it always is, but you only have to do it once. Once you're rolling down the right track just make sure you give it coal every day. You can even miss a day now and then and be fine. The engine is stoked and red hot so if you miss a day of prospecting, if you deprived the engine of coal for just 24 hours it obviously does not come to a screeching stop. You still have your train moving down the tracks at a high rate of speed. You have momentum on your side. The trick is to keep the positive momentum. As long as you don't let the train stop, you have momentum on your side.

So if you have your train moving down the tracks at 50 miles per hour and you go on vacation for a week that means no coal for 5 business days. No problem your train has slowed from 50 miles per hour to 30 miles per hour. You still have momentum on your side so give it coal fast and get back up to speed. As long as you don't let the engine come to a complete stop positive momentum is still working for you. If you're reading this book and you're in sales your goal should be to never let the locomotive stop again. Go on vacation, for sure, just make sure the train is travelling at maximum speed prior to vacation and give it coal quickly when you return.

If you're not in sales the same principle applies to life in general. It's far easier to maintain a routine then to start a new one. So keep your momentum going in your fitness program, weeding your garden, practicing your golf swing, or training your new puppy. Just keep it going. If you let the locomotive of life stop on a regular basis you end up in a slump and it's not a great place to be. Just view a shovel of coal as a positive or happy thought or maybe a good deed. Make sure that you keep the train of life flowing in the proper direction with positive life momentum. Life seems to be on a mission to stop everyone's train, unfortunately it's successful most of the time. Don't be a casualty.

In a nutshell

The people that understand the magic of momentum and the role it plays in our accomplishments can harness the power of positive life momentum. As long as you continue to feed the engine of your life, as long as you apply the necessary coal on a regular basis you will have positive momentum on your side. If you allow the train to stop that's a problem, if you allow the train to stop on a regular basis that could potentially cost you your dreams. Feed your locomotive. I highly recommend you get in the habit of shovelling at least one shovel of coal daily.

Helpful Exercise #12

After reading this chapter you probably realized that there are some areas of your life that could seriously use some positive momentum. The trick is to figure out what provides a shovel of coal in each area. If you're a salesperson the shovel full of coal might be an hour a day making out-bound calls to find new business. As a parent a shovel full of coal might be setting aside time each evening to really listen to your teens. As a community member your shovel of coal might be an hour a week volunteering at the local food bank or driving seniors to medical appointments. Write down three areas of your life in which you would like to have positive momentum and what would represent a shovel full of coal.

Positive area of momentum #1

_____

Shovel full of coal activity

_____

Positive area of momentum #2

_____

Shovel full of coal activity"

_____

Positive area of momentum #3

_____

Shovel full of coal activity

_____

Feed the engine daily.

In the province of the mind

what one believes to be true

is either true or becoming true.

John Lilly

Final Thoughts

Once information has been received you always get to choose what you do with that information. You can implement the ideas into practice, store them away as knowledge, or ignore them completely.

If you take the ideas in this book to heart and implement them, you will ensure lasting change. You can use your new knowledge to chart a new course for your life. You can bring abundance to your side of the fence. Remember, real change takes effort and time. You have to break old habits and form new ones.

The vast majority of people who read books, listen to CDs, and attend seminars really want to change but don't stick with it long enough. They take a few steps in the right direction and then stop, they don't see it through and complete the transition

Step #1   Make the decision to read the book listen to the CD or attend a seminar.

Step #2   Invest the time focus and energy to learn and understand the material and concepts.

Step #3   Implement the necessary structures and procedures to gain the benefits from this newfound path.

Steps #1 and #2 are relatively easy. In fact most business people or anyone interested in self-improvement can accomplish Step #1 and #2 on a regular basis. It's Step #3 that's hard. It's the implementation of our new knowledge that unfortunately more often than not falls by the wayside. It's really a shame.

We hear that, knowledge is power, and think that by gaining the knowledge we are accomplishing something. Unfortunately the truth is if we fail to commit to our new direction, if we don't make the required changes we haven't accomplished anything. Knowledge is not enough. It would be fairer to say that, knowledge is the potential for power. Knowledge will assist you in developing all the required skills and understanding to map out a clear and simple path to the desired result. Knowledge will organize your thoughts and help to create simple easy to follow structures.

Let's stop for a minute and think about basketball. You can learn the rules and history of the game from a book. You can develop an understanding of how to make the perfect jump shot from an instructional video. A good coach can motivate you and run you through drills to improve your skills but that's not the same as playing the game. Knowledge is only the potential for power. You still have to put in your hours on the court. You have to play the game. You have to make mistakes, reflect, and get back into the game. Coaches review games and tweak game plans for the next opponent. There are victories and there are losses. Implementing knowledge into action takes practice. The best players love the game.

So why do people fail? Some fail because they don't take the time to deeply understand key concepts needed to change. They don't possess the required knowledge for success. They fail because while they have a desire to get somewhere in life, they have no clear path to accomplish their desired goals. They can't break it down into steps. This is exactly why most people live their entire lives and never achieve that level of satisfaction for which they long. In this case the failure is due to a lack of knowledge. They didn't know how to achieve a specific goal and therefore find themselves falling short over and over again.

Some people fail even after they have taken the time to learn the path and committed the energy to gain the required skills. They have a clear understanding of what they need to do, but they fail in the implementation stage. This is hard to take. Everyone who has experienced this feels exactly the same way... deeply disappointed with themselves. This happens because true change pushes us outside our comfort zones. If we go too quickly it becomes so uncomfortable, horribly uncomfortable, that we would rather run back to the old ways of doing things. Often when we learn something new it feels really, really, really awkward for a time. If you've had to change your golf swing you know what I mean. You know it's going to help, but it just feels so wrong. Some people can get through this tough implementation stage by themselves but most people need support. That's why my business is not just presenting seminars… it is providing coaching sessions. If you truly want to succeed, you need to build in a support system to help you implement the changes. Who can you talk to?

I would highly recommend that you take all the ideas and thoughts in this book and others, all the thoughts that you think are good ideas. I would highly recommend you take them beyond just things that you agree with and or have some connection with. Take them to the Step #3 the stage of implementation. Take these ideas beyond Step #1 and Step #2 beyond learning and understanding, all the way to the implementation stage. It's time to start living the dream rather than thinking about living the dream.

Have an awesome life.